Chippy

The

Computer Teacher

Vanessa Webbe

Chippy the Computer Teacher

Copyright 2023 @ Vanessa Webbe

A product of Webbewrite Publication
Webbes Ground, Gingerland, Nevis
ISBN: 978-976-96288-78

Registered with CARICOM

Author Contact: webbev3@hotmail.com

Cover Design by Arcquela Bendeito

ABOUT THE BOOK

Chippy the Computer Teacher is written to introduce key concepts about how the computer works and to stimulate interest in computer coding. Chippy, the protagonist in the book, uses a child-friendly conversational tone and condenses complex computer science information into a simplistic form for beginners to understand.

Topics covered in this book include succinct information on hardware and software, application software, networks, the internet, and instructions on how to build a simple website using HTML and CSS. Chippy makes learning about the computer exciting, enticing and unintimidating. An ideal book to motivate children to become advance learners in this era of computer technology.

ACKNOWLEDGEMENTS

All praises to Jehovah God.

I am ever grateful to my daughter Kadeise Hendrickson, for her sterling contribution to the editing of this book. Special 'thank you' to Dr. Thomas Lombardi, who was my Information and Communications Technology (ICT) professor, at the University of the Virgin Islands, for the compulsory ICT course I had to take at business school. Most of the information in this book is the simplified notes from my class with Dr. Lombardi. Dr. Lombardi also assisted in reviewing this work.

Heartfelt thanks and appreciation are also extended to ICT specialist, Francisco Dorset, who zealously assisted with reviewing and editing this book. Sincerest gratitude to all who encouraged, prayed, and supported this work in anyway.

Table of Contents

"Hello, everyone! I am Chippy, the computer.

Some people call me 'Brainy'.

They think I am so smart.

That's because my brain is wired quickly to perform many different tasks to assist my users. Well, it's not exactly a brain like yours.

Can I tell you more about me?

I am made up of four main parts.

A central processing unit, please say CPU, that's kind of like my brain. There is also the monitor. I guess that's my face. That's the screen in front of you, which displays all my features. In other words, it shows the things that I can do. It is also where I display answers to your instructions. A keyboard is also one of my key components. Through the use of a keyboard, I receive instructions from humans, and this is one of the main ways how users communicate with the computer.

A mouse is also used to send instructions. (No, not the one with four legs, that steals cheese).

The mouse I am referring to is a little device connected to the computer that you place on the desk, and it helps you to move around on the computer screen, quickly. You point and click with the mouse.

Sometimes, a printer is connected to me, too, so that you can have the results on paper. But I am very capable of storing information in my memory. Lots, and lots of information. By the way, another name for information is data. In my world, we often use the word 'data'.

In fact, because of all the data I can store, the world is saving a lot of paper, which means saving trees. I help offices to 'go green'. Yippy!

I also come with speakers so that you can enjoy your music and hear all the different sounds I am programmed to produce.

All my body parts are connected by cables. But these days, the wire is not always needed. There are wireless devices as well. I have noticed that these days the world is going 'green' and w ireless.

So let us now list all the different parts I spoke about. These I call my basic parts. No, I don't have private parts like humans, (sorry it's not a biology class). To return to the review, here are the main parts discussed: -

1.The CPU

2. Keyboard

3. Monitor

4. Mouse

5. Speakers

6. Printer

CHIPPY THE COMPUTER TEACHER

CPU   KEYBOARD   MONITOR

MOUSE   PRINTER   SPEAKERS

VANESSA WEBBE

SOME COMMON TYPES OF COMPUTERS

Most of the computers people use at work daily are called personal computers. You know, we don't like long words, so we say PC. Some personal computers are desktop computers. Now, I don't think we need a chip to figure out why they are called desktop computers. Y es, you are correct, to conclude they are called desktop, because the computers fit on desks neatly for users to sit at and work.

Sometimes, I can also be an all-in-one piece, a smaller version of the PC, but still very, very smart. That is what we call a laptop. A smaller version of the laptop is called a tablet computer. You just touch the screen, and it works.

You can easily carry a laptop or tablet from place to place, in your hand or in your bag. I must say, though, it seems like the smaller the device, the easier it is to slip from your hands. Please hold on to your devices carefully! Well, they still get smaller than a tablet. Truthfully, humans have become very smart and have even found a way of installing almost all of me, in a cellphone. And they call the guy a 'smart phone '.

No, the smart phone is not the smartest of us all, not necessarily smarter than I, Chippy, the desktop computer am. It all depends on how we are made and what we are made to d o.

OK, now let's quickly list the other versions of me just discussed. I am a desktop Personal Computer (PC). The other versions of me mentioned were:

1. The laptop
2. The tablet
3. The Smart Phone

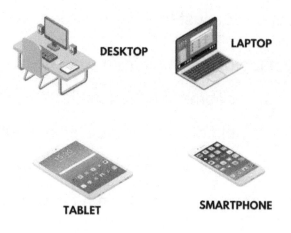

Which type of computer do you prefer?

How do I get to Perform my Work?

So how do I get to perform my work, and to do so quickly? I am designed by humans to do just that. What's ins ide of me? Let's take a look inside my case.

I have a main board, or motherboard, with electrical circuits, which has al l the major connections for me to work. The main circuit is called an integrated circuit. It's also called a microchip, or a chip. A microchip is a very small chip, which is usually 1x1 inch squared in size. It has lots and lots of information and instructions written and programmed on it so that I can know how to function. This chip is further connected to other circuits and wires carrying information. So, now you know why I'm called 'Chippy'!

The chip is a silicon chip. Silicon is an element from the earth that can conduct electricity. I guess you have heard how important silicon has become in our world today. It is so important that places are now named after silicon, like Silicon Valley, which is located in California in the United States. Many leading companies in the field of computer technology are located in Silicon Valley.

HARD SIDE AND SOFT SIDE

Did I tell you that I have a hard side and a soft side? Well, in computer language we say 'hardware' and 'software '.

Ok, so those devices that you see connected to me, like the monitor, keyboard, and the CPU frame, that's hardware. I also have a hard drive inside my case with a bunch of wires connected, that's hardware, too.

Inside my hard drive, I have a system software (that's the soft side) also called an operating system. Now that is what really runs the computer. The most commonly used system software is called Microsoft Windows.

I also have application software. Never mind the term, let me explain. Application software means all the programmes that come with a computer, which you use to get work done.

Examples of application software are programmes like Microsoft Word, Excel, the clock you see, or the games you like to play. The truth is, I can't do much without the application software. Humans use the application software to tell the computer what t o d o. Then t he application software w ill communicate with the system software. The system software knows how to talk to the hardware. The hard drive, the operating system and the application software are inside the frame of the C PU. However, m any applications software t hat a re being used today are available o n t he internet.

This means we are using software that are on other computers that are connected to the internet. We will learn more about network connections a little later in this book. To get back to the discussion on the CPU, we can say, the CPU is always very busy processing information, and does so lickety-split.

Now, for a quick review. What were the hardware and software parts discus sed?

Hardware

Monitor

CPU

Hard drive

Software

Operating System Software

Application Software

MY CAPACITY

The word capacity here means how much work I can do, the speed I can carry out my work, and h ow much information can be stored on my chip. Do you understand? Think of a car and how many persons the car is made to carry. If the car you have in mind is made to carry five persons, then that is the seating capacity of the car.

My memory size will determine how much information can be stored and how fast I can process data.

Computer memory is measured in bits and bytes. A bit is the smallest unit of information that can be stored. The most common unit of storage is a byte, which is made up of 8 bits. In other words, once we have 8 bits together, we change the measuring unit to 1 byte. Then when we have 1024 bytes, we call them all together 1 kilobyte. When we have 1000 kilobytes of data, we c all that 1 megabyte.

Here is a table showing units of measurement in bytes.

Unit	Equivalent
1 byte	8 bits
1 kilobyte (KB)	1024 bytes
1 megabyte (MB)	1,048,576 bytes
1 gigabyte (GB)	1,073,741,824 bytes
1 terabyte (TB)	1,099,511,627,776 bytes
1 petabyte (PB)	1,125,899,906,842,624 bytes

Don't worry so much about the n umbers. Keep in mind that a chip with one megabyte of storage has more memory storage than a chip that has one kilobyte, a gigabyte allows for more memory storage than a megabyte, and a terabyte allows for more storage than a gigabyte and so on. Keep in mind, too, t hat we still have more and more advanced computer c hips being developed that can hold loads and loads and loads of information.

12

The list of bytes goes on and on, to Exabyte (EB), Zettabyte (ZB) and Yottabyte (YB). Now you can sing a byte song to help you to remember the measuring units just mentioned.

How computer information can be stored

Computer information can be stored several ways.

Computer information is stored on a short-term basis in RAM. RAM means Random Access Memory.

RAM stores data temporarily o n t he computer f or programmes that are being used. This therefore means that RAM is usually used when someone is working on a programme on t he computer.

The hard drive is used to store data permanently on the computer. It is always important to save your work when using the computer.

Other ways computer data can be stored include using a USB flash d rive, which is also called a pen drive. Information can also be stored on an external hard drive, that is connected to the computer. In the recent past, computer information was popularly stored on a CD rom. Today, data can also be stored in t he c loud, which means using t he internet to store data.

My Capacity Review

1.What is the smallest unit used to measure computer data?

A. one bit B. one byte C. one kilobyte

Answer: A one bit

2.How many bits make one byte?

Answer: 8 bits equal 1 byte

3.Which computer stores more information?

a) Computer X with a chip of 10 kilobyte

0r

b) Computer Y with a chip of one megabyte.

Answer: B Computer Y with a chip of one megabyte. A megabyte is larger than a kilobyte.

4.What does RAM mean?

Answer: Random Access Memory

5.Name one way computer data can be stored permanently.

Answer: On the hard drive, on the USB drive or in the cloud.

No, computer data is not stored in rain clouds. Storing data in the cloud refers to storing information using the internet.

My Basic Application Software Programmes

Most computers arrive at your door with the following application software that I also have in my system. Some of the most-used application software programmes that come with the Microsoft Windows operating system are:

7-Zip - this helps with the storing of files.

Adobe Reader - some documents are called PDF files. PDF means Portable Document Format. Adobe Reader helps the user to open these documents.

Google Chrome - clicking on Google Chrome opens the door to browse the internet and webpages.

Microsoft Internet Explorer - another software that is used to browse the internet and webpages.

Microsoft Office offers a lot of Microsoft programmes. Some of these are Word, Excel, Power Point and Publisher. These programmes are commonly used by computer users.

Microsoft Windows Media Player - this is actually part o f Windows operating system. Its software allows you to listen music, watch videos and also to store music and videos of your choice.

An Antivirus programme - to protect the computer from getting sick from computer viruses. It can also help to remove viruses from the computer.

The programmes mentioned are for computers using Microsoft Windows. There is another type of computer operating system called Mac for Macintosh made b y the Apple company. This computer system uses similar software as well.

Review - My Basic Software Application Programmes

Many computers come already loaded with the following software application programmes:

Microsoft Windows Operating System

7-Zip

Adobe   Reader

Google Chrome

Microsoft Internet Explorer

Microsoft Office

Microsoft Windows Media Player

An Antivirus

No, you don't have t o worry about y our computer getting SARS o r C OVID-19 virus. No, y our computer does not have t o get vaccinated; instead, it should have an antivirus software for computers. Yes, I guess the antivirus programme is sort of like a vaccine. No, y our computer does not have t o take a shot to install an antivirus software.

COMPUTER CODING

How do we computers know what to do?

We s imply follow instructions that we are programmed to follow. Computers are given a set of instructions to process to make work easier or to help solve problems in shorter time. Writing instructions that tell the computer what to do is called computer programming.

How do we get to understand instructions? Our instructions are written in languages that we understand. No, it's not written in English. No, it's not French or Spanish either, though we can have software with all these languages.

We have our own language, well several languages in which instructions are written that tell us what t o d o. These languages are written by programmers. These are really smart guys and ladies too, w ho love to sit all day and engage in the intricate task of writing programmes for computers. Computer programmers are also called Coders. I think coders are cool.

As I was saying, a computer language is a set of codes used to tell the computer what to do or we can say to provide instructions for the computer. Writing instructions in a computer language is called coding.

Have you ever played a game with a friend that says: when I clap my hands once, it means jump; when I clap my hands twice, it means stop jumping? Well, computer coding is very similar to that game. In fact, o ne of the primary computer coding systems really only works with two numbers, 0 and 1. Because they are only t wo numbers, it i s called a binary number system. Similar to the game you played with your friend, for me the '0' means off and the '1' means on. These numbers tell m e what t o d o. Programmers combine information in binary numbers to provide instructions for u s to follow and we d o just that to perform tasks. A set of instructions that t ell t he computer what t o d o step by step i s called an algorithm.

Apart f rom t he basic binary coding system, there are other computer languages with coding instructions. Some of these languages are:

Java Script, C++, C, Python and Html

Some computer codes are used especially for websites such as Java Script and HTML. HTML means hypertext markup language. Don't get too caught up with the long name. It's ok to just say HTML.

Computer Coding Review.

Writing instructions in a computer language for the computer to follow is called coding.

Some well-known computer programming languages are: -
JavaScript, C++, C, Python and HTML.

Yes, you can explore and learn how to write computer programmes as well. No, you are not too young to learn coding.

At age six, Kautilya Katariya made it to the Guinness World Record for completing IBM'S AI (Artificial Intelligence) certification in 2020. He mastered coding using Python. You can read more about Kautilya on IBM's Developer Blog.

See link below: -

6-year-old Guinness World Record programmer completes IBM AI certification - IBM Developer   -

You, too, can learn more about computer coding. Give it a try and explore!

COMPUTER NETWORKS

Through a network system, I can also talk to other computers.

So, what is a computer network? Ok, that's when two or more computers are linked together and can talk to each other. This means we can share information with each other. Computers and printers connected together on a network are called a set of **nodes.** No, not toads, but nodes. You can underline that w ord.

Here is a picture o f a computer network: -

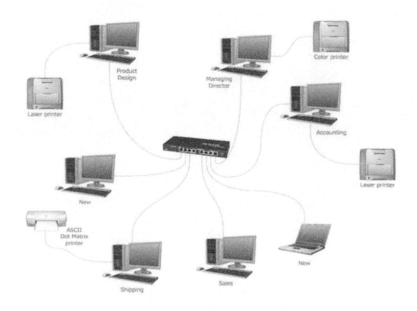

Networks are used in offices and businesses so that employees have access to the same information. Each person is usually given a password to access the network. Not everyone may have access to the same level of information on a network. For instance, the manager will have access to all the information, but an employee may only have access to specific information needed to carry out his or her duties. Some persons may have access to information as necessary.

The disadvantage of a network is that sometimes there might b e a problem that needs fixing, and no one on the job is able to use the computer at that time. Also, computer h ackers can break into a computer network and have access t o important data. Oh, no! We don't want that to happen at all. Saving information on the network in a secure way is very important.

People can connect to a computer network from different locations. This makes it easier for people to work even from home. During the recent Covid-19 pandemic, people were able to work from their homes and remain connected to their workplace computer network. The internet allows many persons to connect on computer networks all over the world.

Computer networks are connected together, too. They are connected together by a device called a router. O k, let us go over that again, to help you to remember: computer networks are connected together b y a router.

More about Networks - LAN and WAN

No, LAN and WAN are not twin brothers.

They are types of computer networks.

LAN means Local Area Network. So then, LAN is a set of computers that are closely linked together, like the computers in one building or the same office. They are in a local area, so we say local area network (LAN).

Perhaps, now you have figured out what is WAN. Yes, it means Wide Area Network. Some computers are connected to each other, although they are far, far away.

What do you think is the largest Wide Area Network? Yes, the Internet!

An IP a ddress

Each computer on a network is given a special label. This label is written in number form, or we can say that it is a numerical label. The numerical label is called an Internet Protocol. But everyone just says an IP address. An IP address that labels a computer may look like this:

192.168.1.1

BANDWIDTH

The amount of data the computer can transfer on a computer network in a given time is referred to as the bandwidth.

Bandwidth is measured in Mbps which means megabits per second. The higher the Mbps the quicker your computer can carry out online activities.

A network bandwidth of 40 Mbps will take longer to download videos from YouTube than that of a network bandwidth of 80 Mbps, which will transfer data two times faster.

The telecommunication companies provide internet services, through their cables that are set up around an island or a country to do just that. These cables are used to transfer data to users.

Network services with a faster speed that can carry more data at a given time, usually cost more to the user. People often choose a plan from the telecommunication company that is workable and affordable.

How fast information moves on a computer network has to do with the bandwidth.

The telecommunication companies provide internet services, through their cables that are set up around an island or a country to do just that. These cables are used to transfer data to users.

Now to Review Networks

So, here I am, your friend Chippy, sitting in an office, with a lovely ocean view. I am a part of a computer network in our building. Along with the printer close by, I am a node on a network. The computers in our building are on a LAN network, a local area network. However, we are connected to the network in another country where we have another business branch. So, we are also a part of a wide area network, WAN. And, like almost all the computers these days, we are connected to the largest WAN, the internet.

In my building, we use cables to connect our network for things to move faster. I have a telephone line cable connected to me which is used to transfer data quickly.

The Internet

I know my users usually log on to the network and the internet. As was mentioned before, more than once, the largest WAN is the internet. I know you know what W AN means by now. Do you know that in 2 012, over 8 billion devices from all over the world, were connected to the internet?

The internet is used to communicate with people all over the world, sending just about any message people want to share. Information is primarily shared through websites.

Websites also include social media platforms such as Facebook and Twitter, which are popularly used. Movies and videos are shown on YouTube channels. People also communicate by sending emails to each other using the internet, for Instant delivery.

The information is also used to promote m any businesses, and for advertising products. People use the internet to buy and sell products. This activity is called e-commerce.

A good question is, w hat is the difference between t he World Wide Web and the internet?

The Internet is all the networks of computers connected together while the World Wide Web is all the webpages found o n all t he computers connected o n the

Internet. So, we can say that the World Wide Web is the soft side, more software stuff, while the Internet is more the hard side, more hardware connections. The World Wide Web, then, is information on webpages found on the internet. But the internet also has other features such as providing communication by emails. Therefore, the World Wide Web is a major feature of the internet, but that is not all to the internet.

I think you get the point.

VANESSA WEBBE

THE INTERNET REVIEW

The internet is the largest WAN network. It is a large network of computers connected together all over the world.

The internet is used to communicate with people all over the globe.

People buy and sell products over the internet. This is called e-commerce. The internet is often used for hosting websites which include social media platforms and YouTube channels. The internet is also used to communicate quickly using emails.

No, World Wide Web is not another name for the internet. The worldwide web is all the websites found on all the computers connected to the internet. The internet has other features apart from websites.

The website Statista.com informs us that as of January 2021, there were 4.66 billion active internet users worldwide, which represents a little more than half of the world's population. No, spiders do not live on the World Wide Web.

CREATING A SIMPLE WEBPAGE
USING HTML

Let us look at building a website using HTML. Firstly, we have to decide what website we will be designing, and for what purpose, and also what information we want to provide to visitors to our site. How about a Website called, 'Wiz Fun Games Club?'

Children will be able to log onto your website and have fun while learning. Ok, let's get going. Open your Chippy, your computer, to a programme called Notepad. You can do a search for it if you are not seeing it on your desktop screen.

We are going to use HTML and what is called CSS coding combined to create a simple website. They tell the computer how to display the webpage. That is why it is called coding! We will type what we call tags. Here are some examples of tags.

<!DOCTYPE html> (that is how we start) <html>

The webpage has a head where we place the

title. <head> (tag to open the head)

<title>write the title here</title>

</head> (tag to close the head)

Next is the body. The information about the website is placed in the body. This portion of information will be displayed to the user.

<body> (tag to open the body)

<h1>My Webpage</h1> (h1 refers to the size of the font. Fonts range from H1 to H6, where H1 is the largest.

We can write paragraphs in the body.

<p> tag to open a paragraph

<p>My webpage is educational and fun. </p>

Pictures and links to other websites can also be inserted in a website. The picture is first saved on the computer, then the instructions
to find the picture are given.

Here is the tag to insert a picture:

<img src="my photo profile.jpg" alt=" My profile photo">

This tells the computer where to find the image or the path to the image.

Here is tag to insert a link to another website: -

<a href="https://www.website link.com">Click here</a>

Here is the closing tag at the end of the body:
</body>

Closing the HTML

</html> this closing tag is used once you have finished designing your webpage.

Now those are some basic tags we will use to create a simple website using HTML coding. Of course, there are lots more features that can be included such as instructions for colours and background, and much more. To further explore you can google tutorials on building websites using HTML and CSS.

Creating the Webpage

Now that we understand some HTML basic coding let's get started in creating our webpage.

Follow the instructions below like a good computer and type exactly what you see on your Notepad.

You can ask questions after.

<!DOCTYPE html>

<html>

```
<head>

<title> Wiz Fun Games Club</title>
</head>

<body>

<h1>Welcome to My Game Page</h1> <p>This is a fun learning page</p>
<h2>Just Click the Link</h2>

<p>You just have to click the link on any game and start playing and
learning. Have fun!</p>
<img src="Mypicture.jpg">alt="My Profile Photo">

<a herf="https://www.funbrain.com/">visit funbrain.com!</a>.


</html>
```
(this means we are closing the html tag so there will be no more html code after this tag).

Now save your work.

Steps to Save:

1.Click file, Save as

2.This PC

3.File name: mywebpage.html

4.Click Save at the bottom of the page.

5.All the files should be saved in the same folder, including your profile photo.

The file will be saved on your desktop. It will look like your internet browser. To view your website, simply click on the file on your desktop. It will open and show you exactly h ow your website will appear on the World Wide Web.

Well done! You are a star student!

We will not be uploading the website live at this introductory stage as this can be a little technical. But you can explore, of course, and get some help to upload your website live on the internet.

MORE ABOUT WEBSITES

All websites have website addresses. A website address gives direction as to how to find your webpage on the World Wide Web. Just like how mail is delivered to your mailing address because you have a definitive address.

For example: John Browne

Stoney Grove

Charlestown, Nevis

Some people may also have house numbers and apartment numbers. I think you have the idea.

So, too, a website address is comprised of different bits of information which is the path to a specific location. A website address is also referred to as a URL which means Uniform Resource Locator.

Here is an example of a basic web address: -

http://www.chippythecomputerteacher.com/chippy.html

The first section of the address highlighted in red is called a protocol. (No, no, it is not connected to the Covid-19 protocol, which you follow carefully to stay safe during the pandemic. Now, this is not a joke). Http stands for Hyper Text Transfer Protocol. Developed in 1989 by Tim Berbers-Lee, the Http protocol carries the rules and guidelines to let other computers know how your website should be displayed. The second part highlighted in blue is referred to as the hostname or domain name.

And the last section of the address highlighted in green is the file name.

The above explanation is given to show in its simplest form how the web address is subdivided.

Generally speaking, a URL has more than three parts, and each part has its own name. I should mention too that .com means commercial. This domain name is available for u se for both commercial and non-commercial websites. Have you noticed how educational institutions use .edu instead of .com. Dot edu, of course, means education, and this allows users to see that an internet address belongs to a school, college or university.

But that's enough on the topic for now.

In the next sequel, we will have a bit more in-depth information on website development and explain further about what each part of the web address is called, and what each part actually means.

So, please, let us take a deep breath and let it out, because that's it on website development for now.

Now put your hands together and give yourself a rousing round of applause for building your first webpage. Kudos to you!

You can proudly fill out the certificate at the back of this book and write the date you created your webpage. How about framing it and placing it on your wall? Sounds like a good idea!

Isn't this fun!

Congratulations!

You are a wiz just like me, your friend Chippy.

Creating a Website Review

1.What is the tag to open the head of a webpage?

Answer: <head>

2. What is the tag to close the head?

Answer: </head>.

3. What is the tag used to close the HTML file?

Answer: </html>

4.What does Http mean?

Answer: Hyper Text Transfer Protocol

5.Which of the following would an educational institution use at the end of the web address?

A .com B. .edu

Answer: B .edu

No, a website address is not information for the postman to know where to deliver letters. A website address allows other computers to locate your website on the World Wide Web.

VANESSA WEBBE

CHIPPY THE COMPUTER TEACHER

Certificate of Award

This Certificate is presented to:

_____

For successfully creating the Wiz Fun Games Club website using Html Coding

You are officially a member of the Chippy computer Club.

Date: _____

A LITTLE COMPUTER HISTORY

•The Z3 is recognised as the first modern computer and was developed by an inventor named Konrad Zuse in 1940.

• In **t he 1940's ,** George Stibitz, one of the fathers of modern digital computers

,

invented "Model K", the first digital computer. It was just a relay-based calculator able to do calculations using simple binary addition.

• **Leonard Kleinrock is credited to have conceptualized the idea of the internet,** after h e published his first paper entitled "Information Flow in Large Communication Nets" on May 31, 1961. T he Internet as we know it today first started being developed in t he l ate 1960s in California in t he United States.

•The silicon chip was invented in 1961 by two American electrical engineers, Jack Kilby and Robert Noyce. Their creation revolutionized and miniaturized technology and paved the way for the development of the modern computer.

• English scientist, Tim Berners-Lee, invented the World Wide Web in 1989.

• Doug Engelbart pioneered the development of the first computer mouse in the early 1960s, which was made of wood.

• Bill Gates founder of Microsoft Windows introduced windows, on November 10, 1998, as a computer operating system that made computer more friendly to use and made the computer more popular.

• Mark Zuckerberg, a former computer science student of Harvard University, along with friends, launched Facebook, the world's most popular social network, in February 2004.

• Twitter was founded by Jack Dorsey, Biz Stone, and Evan Williams Twitter in March 2006.

REFERENCES

Websites:

How to Create a Link With Simple HTML Programming: 9   Steps (wikihow.com)

CSS Tutorial (w3schools.com)

Amazing Facebook Statistics and Facts for 2021 - Market.us

•Internet users in the world 2021 | Statista

ABOUT THE AUTHOR

Vanessa Webbe is a woman of faith who relies on God's help to guide her through every book project. Her genre of writing includes inspirational faith-based books and engaging educational literature for children.

She is the owner of Webbewrite Publication, which also provides a writing service to produce specialized books for businesses and individuals. Ms. Webbe is well known in her community as a poet and playwright.

Residing on the island of Nevis, the smaller of the twin island Federation of St. Kitts and Nevis, Ms. Webbe is a mother of two grown children, Kadeise and Kleeton Hendrickson. She has been gifted with a dorable grandchildren. As a dedicated Christian, Ms. Webbe is passionate about sharing the good news of salvation through outreach evangelism, children's ministry and through her writing. Her hobbies include reading, gardening, and baking.

She is grateful to everyone who impacted her life positively, especially her mother, Bernadine Webbe and her grandfather, the late Daniel Webbe, who raised her in the family home at Cox Village in Nevis.

CHIPPY THE COMPUTER TEACHER

Made in the USA
Columbia, SC
05 June 2023

17381536R00033